Super Easy and Appetizing Stir-fry Cookbook

The Perfect Stir-fry Recipes for Beginners

BY

MOLLY MILLS

Copyright © 2019 by Molly Mills

License Notes

No part of this book may be copied, replicated, distributed, sold or shared without the express and written consent of the Author.

The ideas expressed in the book are for entertainment purposes. The Reader assumes all risk when following any guidelines and the Author accepts no responsibility if damages occur due to actions taken by the Reader.

An Amazing Offer for Buying My Book!

Thank you very much for purchasing my books! As a token of my appreciation, I would like to extend an amazing offer to you! When you have subscribed with your e-mail address, you will have the opportunity to get free and discounted e-books that will show up in your inbox daily. You will also receive reminders before an offer expires so you never miss out. With just little effort on your part, you will have access to the newest and most informative books at your fingertips. This is all part of the VIP treatment when you subscribe below.

SIGN ME UP: *https://molly.gr8.com*

Table of Contents

Perfect Stir-fry Recipes

AAAAAAAAAAAAAAAAAAAAAAAAAAAAAAAAAAAAAAAAAAAAAAAAAA

Recipe 1: Traditional Stir-Fried Chicken

This is a great tasting and easy stir-fried recipe to prepare during the week. It is loaded with vegetables, so feel free to use whatever kind of vegetables you desire. For the tastiest results serve this dish over a bed of white rice.

Yield: 6 Servings

Cooking Time: 1 Hour and 20 Minutes

List of Ingredients:

- 2 Cups of Rice, White in Color
- 4 Cups of Water, Warm
- 2/3 Cup of Soy Sauce, Your Favorite Kind
- ¼ Cup of Brown Sugar, Light and Packed
- 1 tablespoon of Cornstarch
- 1 tablespoon of Ginger, Fresh and Minced
- ¼ teaspoons of Red Pepper Flakes
- 3 Chicken Breasts, Boneless, Skinless and Sliced Thinly
- 1 tablespoon of Oil, Sesame Variety
- 1 Green Bell Pepper, Cut into Small Pieces
- 1 Can of Chestnuts, Water Variety and Drained
- 1 Head of Broccoli, Cut into Small Florets
- 1 Cup of Carrots, Finely Sliced
- 1 Onion, Cut into Small Chunks
- 1 tablespoon of Oil, Sesame Variety

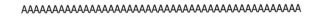

AAAAAAAAAAAAAAAAAAAAAAAAAAAAAAAAAAAAAAAAAAAAAAAAAA

Instructions:

1. First boil your water and rice together for the next 20 to 25 minutes or until your rice is completely tender or until all of your rice has been absorbed.

2. Then use a small sized bowl and combine your next 3 ingredients until smooth in consistency. Mix in your next 3 ingredients, stirring again to combine. Place your chicken into the bowl and toss to coat. Place into your fridge to marinate for the next 15 minutes.

3. Then heat up your oil in a large sized wok placed over medium to high heat. Once the oil is hot enough add in your next 5 ingredients and cook until everything is tender. Remove from wok and set aside.

4. Place your marinated chicken into your wok and cook over medium t high heat. Once your meat is fully cooked through add in your vegetables and marinade and continue cooking for the next 5 to 10 minutes. Remove from heat and serve over a bed of rice.

Recipe 2: Stir Fried Style Veggies and Rice

This is an easy rice and veggies recipe that you are going to want to make to pair excellently with any other stir fried dish that you make. Keep in mind that this dish uses peanut oil, so for those who suffer from peanut allergies should use vegetable oil instead.

Yield: 4 Servings

Cooking Time: 35 Minutes

List of Ingredients:

- 1 ½ Cups of Broth, Vegetable Variety
- ¾ Cup of Rice, White in Color and Uncooked
- 1 tablespoon of Butter, Soft
- 1 tablespoon of Sesame Seeds, Toasted Lightly
- 2 Tablespoons of Oil, Peanut Variety
- ½ Pound of Asparagus, Trimmed and Cut into Small Pieces
- 1 Red Bell Pepper, Cut into Small Pieces
- 1 Onion, Yellow in Color, Large in Size and Sliced Thinly
- 2 Cups of Mushrooms, Finely Sliced
- 2 teaspoons of Ginger, Root, Fresh and Minced
- 1 teaspoon of Garlic, Minced
- 3 Tablespoons of Soy Sauce, Your Favorite Kind
- 1 tablespoon of Oil, Sesame Seed Variety

AAAAAAAAAAAAAAAAAAAAAAAAAAAAAAAAAAAAAAAAAAAAAAAAAA

Instructions:

1. The first thing that you want to do is preheat your oven to 350 degrees.

2. While your oven is heating up, use a medium sized saucepan and combine your first 3 ingredients together. Cover and bring this mixture to a boil. Once the mixture is boiling reduce your heat and allow to cook for the next 15 minutes.

3. Then place your sesame seeds onto a small sized baking sheet and bake in your oven for the next 5 minutes or until light golden brown in color. Remove and set aside.

4. Next heat up your oil in a large sized wok placed over medium to high heat then add in your ginger and garlic. Stir fry this for the next 5 minutes or until your vegetables are tender. Add in your soy sauce and stir thoroughly to coat and cook for the next 30 seconds.

5. Remove from heat and add in your oil and sesame seeds. Stir thoroughly to combine and serve over a bed of rice.

Recipe 3: Classic Beef Stir Fry

If you are looking for a tasty dish that is packed full of flavor, then this is the perfect recipe for you. Packed with healthy veggies and swimming in a delicious garlic sauce, this is one dish you won't be able to help but enjoy.

Yield: 4 Servings

Cooking Time: 1 Hour and 10 Minutes

List of Ingredients:

- 2 Cups of Rice, Brown in Color
- 4 Cups of Water, Warm
- 2 Tablespoons of Cornstarch
- 2 teaspoons of Sugar, White in Color
- 6 Tablespoons of Soy Sauce, Your Favorite Kind
- ¼ Cup of Wine, White in Color
- 1 tablespoon of Ginger, Fresh and Minced
- 1 Pound of Beef Steak, Cut into Small Strips
- 1 tablespoon of Oil, Vegetable variety
- 3 Cups of Broccoli, Cut into Florets
- 2 Carrots, Fresh and Sliced Thinly
- 1 Pack of Peas, Frozen and Thawed
- 2 Tablespoons of Onion, Finely Chopped
- 1 Can of Chestnuts, Water Variety, Undrained and Finely Sliced
- 1 Cup of Cabbage, Chinese Variety
- 2 Heads of Bok Choy, Large in Size and Finely Chopped
- 1 tablespoon of Oil, Vegetable Variety

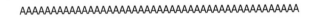

AAAAAAAAAAAAAAAAAAAAAAAAAAAAAAAAAAAAAAAAAAAAAAAAAAA

Instructions:

1. The first thing that you will want to do is cook up your brown rice. To do this bring both your brown rice and your water to a boil in a medium sized saucepan set over high heat. Once your mixture begins to boil reduce the heat to low and allow your rice to cook until completely tender and until the liquid has been fully absorbed. This should take about 45 to 50 minutes.

2. While your rice is cooking, use a small sized bowl and combine your next 4 ingredients together until smooth in consistency. Add in your ginger and toss thoroughly to coat.

3. Then use a large sized wok placed over medium to high heat. Add in your oil and then once it is hot enough add in your next 4 ingredients and stir to combine. Continue cooking for at least a minute.

4. Then add in your next three ingredients and cover. Allow to cook until your vegetables are tender. This should take about 5 minutes. Remove from your pan and set aside to keep warm.

5. Using the same saucepan add in your beef and some oil and continue to cook until your beef is thoroughly brown on all sides. Return your veggies back into your skillet and continue to cook until completely cooked through. Removed and serve over a bed of rice.

Recipe 4: Sesame Style Stir Fried Shrimp

Here is yet another stir fried dish that is incredibly delicious. This is a dish that contains a hint of a nutty flavor and is crispy to taste. I know that after getting a bite of this dish you will want to make it over and over again.

Yield: 4 Servings

Cooking Time: 55 Minutes

List of Ingredients:

- 2 Cups of Water, Warm
- 1 Cup of Rice, White in Color and Uncooked
- 1 Pound of Shrimp, Medium in Size, Peeled and Deveined
- ¼ teaspoons of Ginger, Ground
- ¼ teaspoons of Cayenne Style Pepper
- 1 Cloves of Garlic, Minced
- 1 tablespoon of Sesame Seeds, Lightly Toasted
- ¼ teaspoons of Black Pepper, Ground
- 2 Tablespoons of Oil, Sesame Variety
- 1 Red Bell Pepper, Sliced Into Thin Strips
- 3 Onions, Green in Color and Finely Sliced
- 3 Tablespoons of Teriyaki Sauce, Your Favorite Kind
- ½ Pound of Peas, Sugar Snap Variety
- 1/8 Cup of Cornstarch
- ¾ Cup of Chicken Broth, Homemade Variety
- ¼ teaspoons of Salt, For Taste

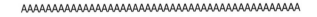

AAAAAAAAAAAAAAAAAAAAAAAAAAAAAAAAAAAAAAAAAAAAAAAAAAA

Instructions:

1. Use a medium sized saucepan and bring your water to a boil. Once the water is boiling add in your rice and allow to simmer for the next 20 minutes.

2. While your rice is cooking combine your next 6 ingredients in a large sized Ziploc bag. Place into your fridge to marinate for the next couple of minutes.

3. Then heat up your oil in a large sized wok placed over medium heat. Once the oil is hot enough add in your next two ingredients and cook for the next 4 minutes or until slightly soft. Then add in your remaining ingredients and stir until thoroughly combined and continue cooking until your shrimp is opaque in color.

4. Season with a dash of salt and serve over your cooked rice.

Recipe 5: Stir Fried Shrimp

Not only is this dish absolutely delicious, but it isn't that difficult to make. The best part about this recipe is that you don't have to be too exact with your measurements.

Yield: 4 Servings

Cooking Time: 30 Minutes

List of Ingredients:

- 1 tablespoon of Salt, For Taste
- 2 Cups of Water, Cold
- 1 Pound of Shrimp, Peeled and Deveined
- 1/3 Cup of Chicken Broth, Homemade Preferable
- 2 teaspoons of Wine, Rice Variety
- 1 ½ teaspoons of Soy Sauce, Your Favorite Kind
- 1 ½ teaspoons of Cornstarch
- ¾ teaspoons of Sugar, White
- 1/8 teaspoons of Pepper, White in Color
- 1 tablespoon of Oil, Vegetable Variety
- 2 Tablespoons of Garlic, Minced
- 1 teaspoon of Ginger Root, Fresh and Minced
- 2 teaspoons of Oil, Vegetable Variety
- 6 Ounces of Snow Peas, With The Strings Removed
- 2 Tablespoons of Chives, Fresh and Finely Chopped
- ¼ teaspoons of Salt

AAAAAAAAAAAAAAAAAAAAAAAAAAAAAAAAAAAAAAAAAAAAAAAAAA

Instructions:

1. Use a large sized bowl and combine your salt and water together. Once stirred add in your shrimp and allow to soak for at least 5 minutes. After this time remove and set to dry on a plate lined with paper towels.

2. Then use a separate small sized bowl and mix together your next 6 ingredients until thoroughly combined. Set aside for later use.

3. Next use a large sized wok and heat it over high heat. Add in your oil and add in your shrimp, making sure to cook until there the shrimp is pink on all sides. This should only take 1 minute.

4. Add in your next 6 ingredients and continue cooking for an additional 5 minutes.

5. Stir your broth into your skillet and cook just until your sauce begins to thicken. Remove from heat and serve right away.

Recipe 6: Cauliflower Style Fried Rice

If you want to enjoy a healthier meal that is low in carbohydrates, then this is the perfect dish for you. It is a classic Chinese recipe that you will want to make over and over again.

Yield: 6 Servings

Cooking Time: 45 Minutes

List of Ingredients:

- 2 Cups of Peas, Frozen and Thawed
- ½ Cup of Water, Warm
- ¼ Cup of Oil, Sesame Variety and Evenly Divided
- 4 Cups of Pork Loin, Cut into Small Cubes
- 6 Onions, Green in Color and Finely Sliced
- 1 Carrot, Large in Size and Cut into Small Cubes
- 2 Cloves of Garlic, Minced
- 20 Ounces of Cauliflower, Finely Shredded
- 6 Tablespoons of Soy Sauce, Your Favorite Kind
- 2 Eggs, Large in Size and Beaten

AA

Instructions:

1. The first thing that you will want to do is stir together your peas and water in a medium sized saucepan. Bring this mixture to a boil before reducing the heat to low. Cook until your peas are tender to the touch. This should take about 5 minutes. After this time drain and set aside.

2. Next place your sesame oil into a large sized wok and set over medium to high heat. Once the oil is hot enough add in your pork and cook until thoroughly brown in color. Once browned transfer your pork to a plate and set aside.

3. Heat up your remaining oil and add in your next 3 ingredients. Cook until tender to the touch. Then add in your cauliflower. Continue to cook for the next 5 minutes.

4. Add in your cooked pork and soy sauce mixture. Continue cooking for the next 3 to 5 minutes or until slightly brown in color.

5. Add in your eggs next and cook until thoroughly scrambled. Remove and serve right away. Enjoy!

Recipe 7: Easy Stir-Fried Tofu and Mixed Veggies

Surprisingly this is one of the easiest stir fried recipes you will come across in this book. With the use of chicken and tofu, you can rest assured that this is a healthy and delicious meal.

Yield: 6 Servings

Cooking Time: 45 Minutes

List of Ingredients:

- 3 Tablespoons of Soy Sauce, light
- 1 teaspoon of Sugar, White
- 1 tablespoon of Cornstarch
- 3 Tablespoons of Wine, Rice and Chinese Variety
- 1 Green Onion, Medium in Size and Finely Diced
- 2 Chicken Breasts, Boneless and Cut into Small Pieces
- 3 Cloves of Garlic, Finely Chopped
- 1 Onion, Yellow in Color and Sliced Thinly
- 2 Green Bell Peppers, Sliced Thinly
- 1 Pack of Tofu, Firm, Drained and Cut into Small Cubes
- ½ Cup of Water, Warm
- 2 Tablespoons of Oyster Sauce, Your Favorite Kind
- 1 ½ Tablespoons of Chili Paste, Mixed with Garlic

Instructions:

1. Use a medium sized bowl and mix together your first 4 ingredients together until thoroughly mixed. Add in your green onions and chicken into your mixture and stir again to combine. Cover with some plastic wrap and allow to marinate for at least 15 minutes.

2. Then set a large sized wok over medium to high heat. Once the oil is hot enough add in your chicken along with your marinade. Cook for the next 5 minutes or until almost done.

3. Add in your next three ingredients and continue to cook for the next 5 minutes, making sure to stir as you do so until your vegetables are tender.

4. Then add in your remaining ingredients and stir thoroughly to combine. Cook and continue to stir until completely heated through. Remove from heat and serve right away.

Recipe 8: Thai Style Peanut Smothered Noodles

If you are a vegan or vegetarian, then this is the perfect dish for you. It is vegan friendly dish that is packed full of healthy vegetables that will benefit your body in the long run.

Yield: 4 Servings

Cooking Time: 35 Minutes

List of Ingredients:

- 1 Pack of Spaghetti, Uncooked
- 1 tablespoon of Cornstarch
- 1 Cup of Broth, Vegetable Variety and Homemade
- 1/3 Cup of Peanut Butter, Creamy Variety
- 3 Tablespoons of Soy Sauce, Your Favorite Kind
- 3 Tablespoons of Honey, Raw
- 3 Tablespoons of Brown Sugar, Light and Packed
- 1 teaspoon of Oil, Sesame Variety
- 1 teaspoon of Ginger, Ground
- ¼ teaspoons of Red Pepper, Ground
- 2 Tablespoons of Sake
- 2 Tablespoons of Oil, Vegetable Variety
- 2 Cloves of Garlic, Minced
- 1 Onion, Medium in Size and Finely Chopped
- 1 Cup of Broccoli, Cut into Florets
- 1 Cup of Carrots, Fresh and Finely Sliced
- ½ Cup of Red Bell Pepper, Finely Chopped
- ½ Cup of Peas, Sugar Snap Variety

AAAAAAAAAAAAAAAAAAAAAAAAAAAAAAAAAAAAAAAAAAAAAAAAAAA

Instructions:

1. Fill up a large sized pot with some water seasoned with some salt and bring to a boil over high heat. Once the water is boiling add in your pasta and cook until it is tender to the touch. Remove and drain. Set aside.

2. Then whisk together your next 9 ingredients together and continue to whisk until your cornstarch fully dissolves. Bring this mixture to a boil over medium to high heat. Once the mixture is boiling reduce the heat to low and continue to cook until thick in consistency. This should take about 5 minutes. Set aside and keep warm.

3. Then heat up your vegetable oil in a large sized skillet set over medium heat. Once the oil is hot enough add in your garlic and onion. Cook until tender to the touch. This should take about 5 minutes.

4. Add in your next 4 ingredients and stir to thoroughly combine. Reduce the heat to low and continue to cook until your vegetables are tender to the touch. This should only take about 5 minutes.

5. Add in your pre-made peanut sauce and cooked pasta, tossing thoroughly to coat. Serve right away and enjoy.

Recipe 9: Chinese Style Pork Lo Mein

If you are a fan of traditional Chinese recipes, then I know you are just going to love this recipe. Easy to make and packed full of healthy and nutritious vegetables, this is one dish you are going to want to make over and over again.

Yield: 4 Servings

Cooking Time: 30 Minutes

List of Ingredients:

- 1 Pack of Pasta, Linguine Style
- 1/3 Cup of Soy Sauce, Low in Sodium
- 2 Tablespoons of Vinegar, Rice Variety
- 2 teaspoons of Cornstarch
- 1 teaspoon of Sugar, White
- ½ teaspoons of Oil, Sesame Variety
- 2 Tablespoons of Oil, Canola Variety
- 2 Cups of Peas, Snap Variety
- 1 Onion, Small in Size, Sweet Variety and Finely Chopped
- 12 Ounces of Pork Tenderloin, Cut into Small Strips
- 1 Pack of Mushrooms, White in Color and Finely Sliced
- 1 Red Bell Pepper, Finely Chopped
- 1 Clove of Garlic, Finely Chopped
- ½ teaspoons of Ginger, Fresh and Finely Chopped
- 2 Cloves of Garlic, Finely Chopped
- 3 Onions, Green in Color and Finely Sliced

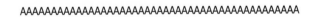
AAAAAAAAAAAAAAAAAAAAAAAAAAAAAAAAAAAAAAAAAAAAAAAAAA

Instructions:

1. The first thing that you want to do is cook your pasta. To do this bring a large sized pot of water to a boil. Once the water is boiling adding your pasta and cook until tender. This should take about 8 to 9 minutes. Once cooked drain your pasta and set aside for later use.

2. Then use a small sized bowl and whisk together your next five ingredients until evenly combined.

3. Next use a large sized skillet and bring over medium to high heat. Add in your oil and then once the oil is hot enough add in your snap peas and onions and cook until soft. This take about 2 minutes. Then add in your next five ingredients and continue to cook until the pork is no longer pink in the middle. This should take about 3 minutes.

4. Add in your pre made sauce over the top of your pork mixture and stir thoroughly until your pork begins to thicken in consistency. Remove from heat and toss in your pasta. Toss thoroughly until fully coated and top off with your green onions. Serve right away and enjoy.

Recipe 10: Shrimp Smothered in Lobster Sauce

If you are a huge fan of seafood, then I know you are going to fall in love with this recipe. For the tastiest results make sure that you use medium to large sized shrimp and serve this dish over a bed of steamed white rice.

Yield: 4 Servings

Cooking Time: 30 Minutes

List of Ingredients:

- 1 ½ teaspoons of Cornstarch
- 2 teaspoons of Sherry, Cooking Variety
- 1 Pound of Shrimp, Medium in Size, Peeled and Deveined
- 4 Tablespoons of Oil, Vegetable Variety
- 2 Cloves of Garlic, Minced
- ¼ Pound of Pork, Ground and Lean
- 1 Cup of Water, Warm
- 2 Tablespoons of Soy Sauce, Your Favorite Kind
- ¼ teaspoons of Sugar, White
- ½ teaspoons of Salt, For Taste
- 1 ½ Tablespoons of Cornstarch
- ¼ Cup of Water, Warm
- 1 Egg, Large in Size and Beaten

AAAAAAAAAAAAAAAAAAAAAAAAAAAAAAAAAAAAAAAAAAAAAAAAA

Instructions:

1. Use a medium sized bowl and dissolve your cornstarch in your sherry. Stir until fully dissolved. Add in your shrimp and toss thoroughly to coat.

2. Heat up some oil in a large sized wok set over medium to high heat. Once the oil is hot enough add in your shrimp and cook until your shrimp turns pink. This should take about 5 minutes. Remove your shrimp and drain on a plate lined with paper towels.

3. Next add your garlic to your wok and continue to cooking for at least 30 seconds. Then add in your pork and cook until your pork no longer is no pink.

4. Add in your next 4 ingredients into your wok and stir to combine.

5. Allow your mixture to come to a boil and then reduce the heat to low. Allow to cook for at least 2 minutes.

6. Add in your remaining ingredients along with your cooked shrimp and continue to cook for the next 7 to 8 minutes. Remove from heat and serve over a bed of rice.

Recipe 11: Spiced Orange Beef

While this is a dish that may sound far from appetizing, once you get a bite I know that you will fall in love with it. This is a great dish to make if you are looking to enjoy a flavorful meal.

Yield: 4 Servings

Cooking Time: 2 Hours

List of Ingredients:

- 1 Pound of Tenderloin, Beef Variety and Cut into Small Strips
- ¼ Cup of Orange Juice, Fresh
- ¼ Cup of Vinegar, Seasoned Rice Variety
- 2 Tablespoons of Soy Sauce, Your Favorite Kind
- 1 tablespoon of Chile Paste, Hot in Flavor
- 1 tablespoon of Brown Sugar, Light and Packed
- 2 Cloves of Garlic, Minced
- ¼ Cup of Water, Warm
- 1 teaspoon of Cornstarch
- Some Cooking Spray
- 2 Tablespoons of Orange Zest, Finely Grated
- 1 Bunch of Green Onion, Finely Sliced and Green and White Parts Separated
- Dash of Salt and Black Pepper for Taste

AAAAAAAAAAAAAAAAAAAAAAAAAAAAAAAAAAAAAAAAAAAAAAAAAA

[38]

Instructions:

1. The first thing that you will want to do is combine your first 7 ingredients into a large sized bowl, making sure to stir thoroughly to combine. Cover with some plastic wrap and place into your refrigerator to chill for at least one to two hours.

2. After this time remove your beef and drain over a colander, making sure to reserve your marinade.

3. Add in your water and cornstarch into your marinade and whisk thoroughly until your cornstarch is fully dissolved. Set this mixture of aside.

4. Next prepare a large sized skillet by greasing it with some cooking spray and set over high heat. Add in your beef and cook for the next minute without stirring it. After this time stir and allow to cook for an additional minute.

5. Add in your green onions and orange zest and continue to cook for the next 30 seconds.

6. Add in your marinade and green onions and cook until your beef it's fully cooked through with no pink showing. Cook for the next 5 minutes or until your mixture is thick in consistency.

7. Season with some salt and pepper and serve right away.

Recipe 12: Lime Flavored Tofu Stir Fry

This is a great dish that you can make whenever you are looking to enjoy something sweet. For the tastiest results I highly recommend letting your tofu marinate for a couple of minutes before cooking it.

Yield: 4 Servings

Cooking Time: 30 Minutes

List of Ingredients:

- 2 Tablespoons of Oil, Peanut Variety
- 1 Pack of Tofu, Extra Firm and Cut into Small Pieces
- 1 tablespoon of Ginger, Minced and Fresh
- 2 Tablespoons of Curry Paste, Red in Color
- 1 Pound of Zucchini, Finely Diced
- 1 Red Bell Pepper, Finely Diced
- 3 Tablespoons of Lime Juice, Fresh
- 3 Tablespoons of Soy Sauce, Your Favorite Kind
- 2 Tablespoons of Maple Syrup, Your Favorite Kind
- 1 Can of Milk, Coconut Variety
- ½ Cup of Basil, Fresh and Roughly Chopped

AAAAAAAAAAAAAAAAAAAAAAAAAAAAAAAAAAAAAAAAAAAAAAAAAA

Instructions:

1. Heat up your peanut oil in a large sized wok set over high heat. Add in your tofu and continue to cook until thoroughly brown in color. Remove and set aside for later use.

2. Add in some more oil to your wok and add in your next two ingredients. Cook until golden color. Then add in your remaining ingredients, making sure to stir thoroughly to combine.

3. Allow to cook for a few minutes or until your vegetables are completely tender.

4. Add in your cooked tofu and toss to combine. Continue cooking until completely heated through. Remove from heat and serve right away.

Recipe 13: Springfield Style Cashew Chicken

This is a world famous dish that originated in the streets of Missouri. To get the tastiest result make this dish alongside some fried rice to make a hearty meal that will leave you feeling completely satisfied.

Yield: 8 Servings

Cooking Time: 55 Minutes

List of Ingredients:

- ½ Quart of Oil, Vegetable Variety and For Frying
- ½ Quart of Oil, Peanut Variety and For Frying
- 1 Egg, Large in Size
- 2 Tablespoons of Water
- 1 ½ Cups of Flour, All Purpose Variety
- 3 Pounds of Chicken Breasts, Boneless and Cut into Small Cubes
- 3 Cups of Water, Warm
- 5 Tablespoons of Cornstarch
- 6 Bouillon Cubes, Chicken Variety
- 2 Tablespoons of Oyster Sauce
- Some Pepper, White in Color and For Taste
- 1 Cup of Cashews, Your Favorite Kind
- 1 Cup of Onions, Green in Color

AAAAAAAAAAAAAAAAAAAAAAAAAAAAAAAAAAAAAAAAAAAAAAAAAA

Instructions:

1. The first thing that you will want to do is heat up your oil in a deep fryer or a large sized wok until piping hot. Then preheat your oven to 200 degrees.

2. Then beat together your egg with at least two tablespoons of water in a small sized bowl and set aside.

3. Place your flour into a separate small sized bowl and set aside.

4. Next take your chicken cubes and dip them first into your egg mixture and then roll them in your flour until completely coated.

5. Place your coated chicken into your hot oil and fry until your chicken is golden brown in color. This should take at least 6 to 8 minutes.

6. While your chicken is cooking whisk together your next five ingredients in a small sized sauce pan and cook for the next 5 minutes or until your mixture is thick in consistency. Remove and set aside.

7. Once all of your chicken has been cooked pour sauce over the top and garnish with your green onions and cashews. Serve right away and enjoy.

Recipe 14: Panang Style Curry Chicken

This is a classic recipe in Thailand and is considered a delicacy in many places. Feel free to add whatever kind of additional ingredients you wish to make it something truly unique.

Yield: 4 Servings

Cooking Time: 35 Minutes

List of Ingredients:

- 5 Tablespoons of Curry Paste, Panang Style
- Some Cooking Oil, Vegetable Variety
- 4 Cups of Milk, Coconut Variety
- 2/3 Pound of Chicken Breasts, Skinless, Boneless and Cut into Small Cubes
- 2 Tablespoons of Sugar, Palm Variety
- 2 Tablespoons of Fish Sauce
- 6 Lime Leaves, Kaffir Variety and Roughly Torn
- 2 Chili Peppers, Fresh, Red in Color and Finely Sliced
- ¼ Cup of Basil Leaves, Thai Style and Fresh

AAAAAAAAAAAAAAAAAAAAAAAAAAAAAAAAAAAAAAAAAAAAAAAAA

Instructions:

1. Fry up your curry paste in some oil in a large sized wok placed over medium to high heat.

2. Then add in your coconut milk and bring your mixture to a boil. Once boiling add in your chicken and continue to cook until completely cooked through. This should take about 10 to 15 minutes.

3. Stir in your next 4 ingredients and allow to come to a simmer for the next 5 minutes. Taste and add some more seasoning if you wish. Remove from heat and garnish with your remaining two ingredients and serve right away.

Recipe 15: Szechwan Style Shrimp

While at first this may seem like a hard dish to make, don't worry. It is actually very simple and one of the best recipes to make if you are looking to bring a little spice to your kitchen. For the tastiest results I highly recommend serving this dish on top of a bed of rice.

Yield: 4 Servings

Cooking Time: 20 Minutes

List of Ingredients:

- 4 Tablespoons of Water, Warm
- 2 Tablespoons of Ketchup, Your Favorite Kind
- 1 tablespoon of Soy Sauce, Low in Sodium
- 2 teaspoons of Cornstarch
- 1 teaspoon of Honey, Raw
- ½ teaspoons of Red Pepper, Crushed
- ¼ teaspoons of Ginger, Ground
- 1 tablespoon of Oil, Vegetable Variety
- ¼ Cup of Onions, Green in Color and Finely Sliced
- 4 Cloves of Garlic, Minced
- 12 Ounces of Shrimp, Fully Cooked and With Tails Removed

AAAAAAAAAAAAAAAAAAAAAAAAAAAAAAAAAAAAAAAAAAAAAAAAAA

Instructions:

1. Use a medium sized bowl and stir together your first 8 ingredients until thoroughly combined. Set aside for later use.

2. Then heat up your oil in a large sized skillet placed over medium to high heat. Once the oil is hot enough add in your green onions and garlic and continue to cook until your garlic is fragrant. This should take about 30 seconds to 1 minute.

3. Add in your shrimp, making sure to toss thoroughly to coat and add in your pre-made sauce. Cook until your sauce is thick in consistency. Remove and serve right away.

Recipe 16: Pancit Style Shrimp

This is a traditional Filipino Recipe that you will quickly fall in love with. It is extremely easy to make and incredibly delicious. I guarantee that it will please the pickiest of eaters.

Yield: 4 Servings

Cooking Time: 40 Minutes

List of Ingredients:

- 1 Pack of Noodles, Rice Variety
- 5 Tablespoons of Oil, Vegetable Variety and Evenly Divided
- 1 Onion, Small in Size and Minced
- 2 Cloves of Garlic, Minced
- ½ teaspoons of Ginger, Ground
- 1 ½ Cups of Shrimp, Small in Size, Fully Cooked and Diced Finely
- 1 ½ Cups of Pork, Fully Cooked and Chopped Roughly
- 4 Cups of Bok Choy, Roughly Shredded
- 3 Tablespoons of Oyster Sauce
- ¼ Cup of Chicken Broth, Homemade Preferable
- ¼ teaspoons of red Pepper Flakes, Crushed
- 1 Onion, Green in Color and Minced

AAAAAAAAAAAAAAAAAAAAAAAAAAAAAAAAAAAAAAAAAAAAAAAAAA

Instructions:

1. The first thing you want to do is soak your noodles in some water for at least 20 minutes. After this time drain it.

2. Then heat up your oil in a large sized wok set over medium to high heat. Once your oil is hot enough add in your noodles and cook for at least one minute. Remove and keep warm.

3. Then add some more oil to your wok and your next five ingredients and continue to cook for a couple of minutes.

4. Add in your next three ingredients and season with your pepper flakes. Stir thoroughly to combine.

5. Cover and allow to cook for an additional minute or until your bok choy is fully wilted. Spoon the mixture over your noodles and garnish with your green onions. Enjoy.

Recipe 17: Sweet and Sour Style Pork

This is a great tasting recipe that makes for the perfect lunch or dinner dish. The real secret behind this dishes great taste is the apple cider vinegar and I guarantee that once you get a bite of it, you won't be able to stop eating it.

Yield: 4 Servings

Cooking Time: 2 Hours

List of Ingredients:

- 1 Pork Butt, Cut into Small Pieces
- 1 teaspoon of Salt, For Taste
- ¼ teaspoons of Sugar, White in Color
- 1 teaspoon of Soy Sauce, Your Favorite Kind
- 1 Egg White, Large in Size
- 2 Onions, Green in Color and Finely Chopped
- 1 Quart of Vegetable Oil, For Frying Only
- ½ Cup of Cornstarch
- 1 tablespoon of Oil, Vegetable Variety
- 3 Stalks of Celery, Cut into Small Pieces

- 1 Green Bell Pepper, Cut into Small Pieces
- 1 Onion, Medium in Size and Cut into Small Wedges
- Some Sugar, White I Color and For Taste
- Dash of Salt, For Taste
- 1 Cup of Water, arm
- ¼ teaspoons of Salt, For Taste
- ¾ Cup of Sugar, White in Color
- 1/3 Cup of Vinegar, Apple Cider Variety
- ¼ Cup of Ketchup, Your Favorite Kind
- ½ teaspoons of Soy Sauce, Your Favorite Kind
- 1 Can of Pineapple, Chunky and Undrained
- 2 Tablespoons of Cornstarch
- ¼ Cup of Water, Warm

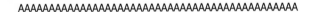

AAAAAAAAAAAAAAAAAAAAAAAAAAAAAAAAAAAAAAAAAAAAAAAAAA

Instructions:

1. Place your pork into a medium sized bowl and season with your first 4 ingredients. Stir thoroughly to combine.

2. Add in your next ingredient along with green onions and toss again to combine. Cover with some plastic wrap and place into your fridge for at least an hour.

3. Meanwhile heat up your oil in a large sized saucepan until piping hot.

4. Add in your coated pork and drop into your oil and cook for the next 10 minutes. After this time remove and drain on a plate lined with some paper towels.

5. Then heat up some oil in a large sized wok placed over medium heat. Once hot add in your next three ingredients and cook until soft and tender. Season with some salt and sugar and remove from heat. Set aside for later use.

6. Next use a large sized saucepan and combine the remaining ingredients including your cooked pork and bring the mixture to a boil. Add in some water and cornstarch and cook until the sauce is thick in consistency. Remove from heat and serve.

Recipe 18: Eggplant Smothered in Garlic Sauce

This is a hearty dish with a slight kick to it. It is incredibly healthy yet contains the perfect amount of spice that I know you won't be able to resist.

Yield: 6 Servings

Cooking Time: 25 Minutes

List of Ingredients:

- 3 Tablespoons of Oil, Canola Variety
- 4 Eggplants, Chinese Variety and Cut into Small Pieces
- 1 Cup of Water, Warm
- 1 tablespoon of Red Pepper Flakes
- 3 Tablespoons of Garlic, Powdered
- 5 teaspoons of Sugar, White in Color
- 1 teaspoon of Cornstarch
- 2 Tablespoons of Soy Sauce, Light
- 2 Tablespoons of Oyster Sauce

Instructions:

1. Heat up your canola oil in a large sized wok placed over medium to high heat.

2. Add in your eggplant and cook until soft. Then add in your next three ingredients and stir to combine. Cover and allow your mixture to simmer until all of the water has been fully absorbed.

3. While your mixture is simmering use a medium sized bowl and mix together your next 4 ingredients until your cornstarch and sugar fully dissolves.

4. Stir the sauce into your eggplant mixture and toss thoroughly to coat. Cook just until your sauce is thick in consistency and remove from heat and serve.

Recipe 19: Classic Beef and Broccoli

If you are a huge fan of beef and broccoli that you can get from any local Chinese restaurant, then this is the perfect recipe for you. Not only is this dish incredibly easy to make, but it tastes absolutely delicious as well. For the tastiest results, make sure that you serve this dish over a bed of white rice for the tastiest results.

Yield: 4 Servings

Cooking Time: 1 Hour

List of Ingredients:

- 1/3 Cup of Oyster Sauce
- 2 teaspoons of Oil, Sesame Variety and Lightly Toasted
- 1/3 Cup of Sherry
- 1 teaspoon of Soy Sauce, Your Favorite Kind
- 1 teaspoon of Sugar, White in Color
- 1 teaspoon of Cornstarch
- ¾ Pound of Beef Steak, Cut into Small Strips
- 3 Tablespoons of Oil, Vegetable Variety
- 1 Piece of Ginger, Fresh and Thinly Sliced
- 1 Clove of Garlic, Smashed
- 1 Pound of Broccoli, Cut into Small Florets

AAAAAAAAAAAAAAAAAAAAAAAAAAAAAAAAAAAAAAAAAAAAAAAAAAAA

Instructions:

1. First whisk together your first 6 ingredients in a large sized bowl and stir until your sugar has fully dissolved. Place your steaks into this bowl and stir well to coat. Cover with some plastic wrap and place into your refrigerator for the next 30 minutes.

2. Then heat up your oil in a large sized wok and place over medium to high heat. Once the oil is hot enough add in your ginger and garlic and cook for the next couple of minutes. Remove and add in your broccoli, making sure to stir thoroughly to coat. Cook for the next 7 minutes or until tender to the touch. Remove from your wok and set aside.

3. Then add in some more oil and your coated beef and cook for the next 5 minutes or until your beef is no longer pink. Return your veggies back to your wok and stir to combine. Continue to cook for the next 5 minutes or until completely cooked through. Remove and serve on top of a bed of rice. Enjoy.

Recipe 20: Stir Fried Tofu and Peanuts

If you are going to eat tofu, then this is the best way to do it. The tofu that you will use in this recipe has a crunchy exterior while still having a soft inside. It is a delicious dish to make that doesn't cost much to prepare. I know you are going to love it.

Yield: 8 Servings

Cooking Time: 30 Minutes

List of Ingredients:

- 1 teaspoon of Oil, Vegetable Variety
- 1 Pack of Vegetables, Stir Fried Variety and Frozen
- ½ teaspoons of Ginger, Fresh and Minced
- Dash of Salt and Pepper, For Taste
- 2 Eggs, Large in Size and Beaten
- 1 Cup of Cornstarch
- Dash of Salt and Pepper, For Taste
- 1 Pack of Tofu, Firm, Drained and Cut into Cubes
- ½ Cup of Oil, Vegetable Variety
- ¾ Cup of Peanut Sauce
- ¼ Cup of Peanuts, Finely Chopped

AAAAAAAAAAAAAAAAAAAAAAAAAAAAAAAAAAAAAAAAAAAAAAAAAA

Instructions:

1. Using a large sized wok, heat up your oil over medium to high heat. Add in your vegetables and cook until tender. Season with a dash of salt and pepper and then remove from skillet and set aside.

2. Then place your eggs into a medium sized bowl and beat thoroughly.

3. Using a separate sized bowl mix together your next 3 ingredients until thoroughly combined. Set aside.

4. Then dip your tofu cubes into your egg mixture first along with your cornstarch mixture.

5. Add in your remaining oil to your wok and heat over medium to high heat. Cook your coated tofu for the next 5 minutes or until all the sides are golden brown in color. Add in your remaining ingredients along with the sautéed vegetables and continue cooking until completely heated through. Remove and serve right away.

Recipe 21: Stir Fried Ginger and Veggies

Here is yet another stir fried recipe that you won't be able to help but enjoy. Feel free to add in some tofu to give this dish a truly unique flavor that you won't be able to resist.

Yield: 6 Servings

Cooking Time: 40 Minutes

List of Ingredients:

- 1 tablespoon of Cornstarch
- 1 ½ Cloves of Garlic, Crushed
- 2 teaspoons of Ginger, Fresh, Finely Chopped and Evenly Divided
- ¼ Cup of Oil, Vegetable Variety and Evenly Divided
- 1 Head of Broccoli, Cut into Small Florets
- ½ Cup of Peas, Snow Variety
- ¾ Cup of Carrots, Cut Julienne Style
- ½ Cup of Green Beans, Cut into Halves
- 2 Tablespoons of Soy Sauce, Your Favorite Kind
- 2 ½ Tablespoons of Water, Warm
- ½ Tablespoons of Salt, For Taste

AAAAAAAAAAAAAAAAAAAAAAAAAAAAAAAAAAAAAAAAAAAAAAAAAAA

Instructions:

1. Use a large sized bowl and combine your first 2 ingredients together until your cornstarch is fully dissolved.

2. Add in your next 4 ingredients together and toss thoroughly to coat.

3. Heat up your oil in a large sized wok placed over medium heat. Add in your vegetables and cook for the next few minutes, making sure to stir constantly.

4. Add in your water along with your remaining ingredients and continue to cook until your vegetables or crispy and tender. Remove answer right away.

Recipe 22: Thai Style Chicken and Basil

If you are looking for a dish with a bit of a kick to it, then this is the perfect recipe for you. Keep in mind this dish is particularly spicier than most so make sure that you have a glass of milk on hand.

Yield: 6 Servings

Cooking Time: 35 Minutes

List of Ingredients:

- 2 Cups of Rice, Jasmine Variety and Uncooked
- 1 Quart of Water, Warm
- ¾ Cup of Milk, Coconut Variety
- 3 Tablespoons of Soy Sauce, Your Favorite Kind
- 3 Tablespoons of Vinegar, Rice Wine Variety
- 1 ½ Tablespoons of Fish Sauce
- ¾ teaspoons of Red Pepper Flakes
- 1 tablespoon of Olive Oil, Extra Virgin Variety
- 1 Onion, Medium in Size and Finely Sliced
- 2 Tablespoons of Ginger, Fresh and Minced
- 3 Cloves of Garlic, Minced
- 2 Pound of Chicken Breast, Skinless, Boneless and Cut into Small Pieces
- 3 Mushrooms, Shiitake Variety, Finely Sliced
- 5 Onions, Green in Color and Finely Chopped
- 1 ½ Cups of Basil Leaves, Fresh and Roughly Chopped

AAAAAAAAAAAAAAAAAAAAAAAAAAAAAAAAAAAAAAAAAAAAAAAAA

Instructions:

1. First thing you want to do is cook your rice. To do this add in your rice and water to a medium sized pot and bring to a boil. Once boiling reduce the heat to low and cook for the next 20 minutes or until the water has been fully absorbed.

2. Then use a medium sized bowl and combine your next 5 ingredients together until thoroughly combined.

3. Using a large sized wok, heat up your oil over medium to high heat. Once the oil is hot enough add in your remaining ingredients and cook for the next 5 minutes. Continue to cook until your sauce has been reduced by at least a third and then remove from heat. Serve over a bed of rice and enjoy.

Recipe 23: Mongolian Style Beef and Onions

This is a classic Chinese style dish that is great for feeding a large group of people. For the tastiest results I highly recommend serving this dish over a bed of rice of noodles.

Yield: 4 Servings

Cooking Time: 30 Minutes

List of Ingredients:

- 2 teaspoons of Oil, Vegetable Variety
- 1 tablespoon of Garlic, Finely Chopped
- ½ teaspoons of Ginger, Fresh and Finely Grated
- ½ Cup of Soy Sauce, Your Favorite Kind
- ½ Cup of Water, Warm
- 1 Pound of Beef Steak, Sliced Into Small Pieces
- ¼ Cup of Cornstarch
- 1 Cup of Oil, Vegetable Variety and For Frying
- 2 Bunches of Onions, Green in Color and Cut into Small Pieces

AA

Instructions:

1. The first thing that you want to do is heat up your oil in a large sized saucepan. Place over medium heat and add in your garlic and ginger and cook for the next 30 seconds.

2. Then add in your next three ingredients and continue to cook for the next 4 minutes or until your sugar has fully dissolved and your sauce is thick in consistency. Remove from heat and set aside for later use.

3. Then place your beef into a large sized bowl and add in your cornstarch. Toss to thoroughly combine. Allow to sit for the next 10 minutes to fully absorb.

4. Then heat up your vegetable oil in a deep large sized wok and place over high heat.

5. Place your beef into your hot oil and cook for the next 2 minutes or until crispy on the outside. Remove and allow to drain on a plate lined with paper towels.

6. Remove the oil from your wok and place your beef back into it. Pouring your pre-made sauce and your remaining ingredients. Stir to combine.

7. Continue cooking over medium heat for the next 2 minutes and remove from heat and serve.

Recipe 24: Thai Style Red Curry Chicken

If you are looking for a dish that is a little spicier, then this is the perfect dish for you. It is relatively easy to make and makes for a great tasting quick meal. It is so delicious that I know you won't be able to resist it.

Yield: 4 Servings

Cooking Time: 20 Minutes

List of Ingredients:

- 2 teaspoons of Olive Oil, Extra Virgin Variety
- 1 Pound of Chicken Breasts, Skinless, Boneless and Cut into Small Strips
- 1 tablespoon of Curry Paste, Thai Variety and Red in Color
- 1 Cup of Zucchini, Cut into Halves and Finely Sliced
- 1 Red Bell Pepper, Seeded and Finely Sliced
- ½ Cups of Carrots, Fresh and Finely Sliced
- 1 Onion, Cut into Quarters
- 1 tablespoon of Cornstarch
- 1 Can of Coconut Milk, Light
- 2 Tablespoons of Cilantro, Fresh and Finely Chopped

AAAAAAAAAAAAAAAAAAAAAAAAAAAAAAAAAAAAAAAAAAAAAAAAAA

Instructions:

1. First heat up some oil in a large sized skillet over medium to high heat. Once the oil is hot enough add in your chicken and cook for the next three minutes.

2. Next mix in your next 5 ingredients and stir to combine. Continue cooking for the next couple of minutes.

3. Then dissolve your cornstarch in your coconut milk until the cornstarch is fully dissolved and pour into your skillet.

4. Bring your mixture to a boil and then reduce the heat to low. Continue cooking for another minute. Remove from heat and serve topped with cilantro. Serve right away and enjoy.

Recipe 25: Garlic Style Chicken

If you are a huge fan of the taste of garlic, then this is the perfect stir-fried dish for you. This is an actual simple stir fried recipe that even the notice cook can easily prepare.

Yield: 4 Servings

Cooking Time: 25 Minutes

List of Ingredients:

- 2 Tablespoons of Oil, Peanut Variety
- 6 Cloves of Garlic, Minced
- 1 teaspoon of Ginger, Fresh and Finely Grated
- 1 Bunch on Onions, Green in Color and Finely Chopped
- 1 teaspoon of Salt, For Taste
- 1 Pound of Chicken Breasts, Boneless, Skinless and Cut into Small Strips
- 2 Onions, Sliced Thinly
- 1 Cup of Cabbage, Finely Sliced
- 1 Red Bell Pepper, Thinly Sliced
- 2 Cups of Peas, Sugar and Snap Variety
- 1 Cup of Chicken Broth, Homemade Variety
- 2 Tablespoons of Soy Sauce, Your Favorite Kind
- 2 Tablespoons of Sugar, White in Color
- 2 Tablespoons of Cornstarch

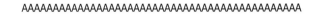

AAAAAAAAAAAAAAAAAAAAAAAAAAAAAAAAAAAAAAAAAAAAAAAAAAA

Instructions:

1. The first thing you want to do is heat up your peanut oil in a large sized wok placed over medium heat. Once your oil is hot enough add in your first 4 ingredients and continue cooking for the next 2 minutes.

2. Add in your chicken and continue to cook for the next 5 minutes. Then add in your next 6 ingredients and stir to combine. Cover.

3. Use a small sized bowl and combine your remaining ingredients together until fully mixed. Pour this over your chicken and vegetables and continue cooking until your sauce is thick in consistency. Remove from heat and serve over a bed of rice.

About the Author

Molly Mills always knew she wanted to feed people delicious food for a living. Being the oldest child with three younger brothers, Molly learned to prepare meals at an early age to help out her busy parents. She just seemed to know what spice went with which meat and how to make sauces that would dress up the blandest of pastas. Her creativity in the kitchen was a blessing to a family where money was tight and making new meals every day was a challenge.

Molly was also a gifted athlete as well as chef and secured a Lacrosse scholarship to Syracuse University. This was a blessing to her family as she was the first to go to college and at little cost to her parents. She took full advantage of her college education and earned a business degree. When she graduated, she joined her culinary skills and business acumen into a successful catering business. She wrote her first e-book after a customer asked if she could pay for several of her recipes. This sparked the entrepreneurial spirit in Mills and she thought if one person wanted them, then why not share the recipes with the world!

Molly lives near her family's home with her husband and three children and still cooks for her family every chance she gets. She plays Lacrosse with a local team made up of her old teammates from college and there are always some tasty nibbles on the ready after each game.

Don't Miss Out!

Scan the QR-Code below and you can sign up to receive emails whenever Molly Mills publishes a new book. There's no charge and no obligation.

Sign Me Up

https://molly.gr8.com